THE GARDEN
OF EPICURUS

by

James Magorian

☙

THE IBIS PRESS
Chicago

"A LARGE rose-tree stood near the entrance of the garden: the roses growing on it were white, but there were three gardeners at it, busily painting them red."
— Lewis Carroll

CONTENTS

[*vii*]

THE GARDEN OF EPICURUS

THE DEER

thick dark clouds
   breaking
      into strips
      of blue
brown rocks
protruding
from steep slopes
      pine needles
      pine cones
across a narrow ravine
a deer moves
into deep timber
   a squirrel chatters
         danger signals
afternoon wind
    bending
        trees
        dry grass
bones of a deer
   white
     against
   brown pine needles
all there
    except
    the skull
somewhere
nailed above
a fireplace

THE GIFT

a bold tremendous stare
elegant with wrath
    carved with care
howling mystery
    marked
for the same tomorrow
    angels fleshed
    from wounded stars
    living
    in cheap hotels
    and empty bars
delirious mentor
    talking in cheers
    selling torches
    keeping treasure
    in antique confusion
knowledge shoved into names
    in folding delusion
private language
measured war
caged war
    warned and removed
because of the holidays
    forgotten
    into sharp stones
    growing from graves
fabled visitors
forgiven child
    simple

and wild
absolute love
ashes beyond pride
the idle temple
where anger died
the last
bleeding sound
anonymous
in caves found
below the gaze
of accidents
imaged and sold
streaming tugging dreaming
wrapped in gold
twilight signs
sources of conspiracy
sudden cradle
visions written down
before the sea arrived
ashamed
elements crowned
falling legends
dying of justice
the last
slow resolve
hid in honesty
praising terror
names columned
in fear
flesh palaced
growing and ringing
fashion weeded
ambition seeded

                    shattered evil
          perfected in the hills
                    sky-wish
                    eyesight cubed
          the required fear
          plunged into stone
                    what victims
                    what victims
          aristotle broken
          and guilty
                    how far
          three nickels
          and a bus token
          that's how far
               volumes bound
               but never found
          charades of suffering
               glorious songs
               glittering roads
          dungeon walls
          screaming halls
                    invading armies
                         of beggars
               moonlit birth
               last birth
                    crusader eyes
                         raging
                    over the edge
                    of a plagiarized shield
          vengeance distributed
          ruins agreed upon

SO MANY

so many symbols born
    of fact
and fed
    on fear

so many angles
    shaped by sound
for none
    to hear

so many faded festivals
    of fame
drawing crowds
    toward a name

so many tongues
    turned
in timeless music
the newest songs found
    and learned

so many particles
    of knowledge
that never touch
    or teach

so many beginnings
    with ends
beyond reach

so many numbers subtracted
    from the whole
to slowly counterfeit
    a soul

EVERY DIRECTION

in familiar hills
where my feet
walk with lame gait
through ravines where
coyotes sit and wait
dirt carpenters
in white sun helmets
have started
to excavate my mind
digging
shifting
changing every substance
supporting every doubt
inventing ancient lands
small sharp tools
clutched in academic hands
rearranging rules
losses and gains
memories and hopes
marked out
with wooden stakes
and rough ropes
in the shadows

of 4-wheel-drive trucks
loaded with boxes
and shovels
chronologies constructed
blind children
carefully instructed
piles of stones
designed with caution
buffalo bones
removed from prairie graves
brushed with shellac
labeled with numbers
carried back
to dark pipesmoke rooms
examined
and placed in museums
i close my eyes
seal my mind with sadness
and hobble past
shackled in silver-hammered
chains

STORM

wind moves
low clouds
to conceal
solemn sun

calendars
of leaves
turn dark
with fear

creations
wash away
parallels
from time

no guilt
invented
no cause
examined

shadows
through
a sieve
of love

at noon
an echo
invades
a death

rainbow
rafters
release
the sky

separate
universe
scatters
colonies

the end
returns
a dream
in rain

THE LIMITS OF CELEBRATION

the fanfare
of decorated
events
(reaching toward
the corner
of dollar bills)
is careful
not to touch
the burning
birthday cake
candles
pointing skyward
to greedy wishes
(surrounded by gifts
without givers)
lost somewhere
in the war cries
nicely curious
(but not the publicity
that was sought)
and sustained
by negative breath
of old reasons

IF VOICES

"Mankind is tolerant of the praises of others so long
as each hearer thinks he can do as well or nearly as
well for himself, but when the speaker rises above him,
jealousy is aroused and he begins to be incredulous."
— Thucydides

words   only half there
   and besides
   what's
a name here and there
     manufactured significance
   that
     doesn't cancel death
so   where
    does when begin

what
   is truth
     beyond
       survival instincts
   the gains
    are
   losses
but   those
  things   not what
    they seem

is there a pawnshop
   for a broken dream

wandering senses
plotting tenses
   was and were
   is and be

crawling
        back
    into the sea
having chopped down
    the last tree

the low lingering heartbeat of fools
                this
luck

only a mixture of molecules
        that clothing
            the wrong pause
a slandering blast of rushing rules

then
        they will
            remember
        the times
when

A LION WINKS

       victims
joyous in defeat
wildly cheering
the last refusal
to retreat

       mold
voices in song
to kill thought
with raw noise
and hide a wrong

     broken song
of bold decision
floating westward
with soft speed
and cold precision

     preparing
a slow sacrifice
evil and exact
to solemnly honor
ignorant advice

                angles
where motions meet
divide the roads
silently trod
by holy feet

                wheels
tear the ground
with wounded
weights and bursts
of sound

                particles
of dull blue sky
merge in patterns
of pure anger
and quickly die

                all gods
have now departed
for new homes
along routes
still uncharted

MORNING IN THE GARDEN OF EPICURUS

darkness
wind
spires
of summer grass
shadows shifting
with the wind
on a moon-generous night
animals wandering
  crying
  calling
in the night
looking for the ark
  glowing eyes
  candles of fear
lurking in the shadows
of small silent sheds
stalking across empty poultry-yards
  over rolls of wire
leaning against naked fence posts
across rough-ploughed fields
through tall thick bushes
into the caves of night
  gone
leaving a mud-told tale
along the stream
  gone
as morning appears
with the privileges
  of red
given in the east

creaking haunted towers
black shaking towers
become mulberry trees
   apricot trees
   walnut trees
   apple trees
gifts of sun and rain
in a holy land
a fortress of wild roads
   spreading dust
   on unknown maps
great songs of mysterious intervals
long hopes of grape vines
green tides of corn
fed by primordial mixtures
      insolent images
separation and recall
all visions narrowed
by the angles
of memory
and the laugh
of night
   now expand
      with the spin
      of the earth
cool mist
glimmering dew
swords of light
cutting through the land
arriving to save
   reality from myth

climbing vines
with orange crowns
      above rose bushes
      above secretly traveled paths
cool in the witness-shade
of an olive tree
    cautious
around the corners
of mock war
morning
time
self
are all one
and belong
to wind
and sun
    quiet
in morning breezes
flower-rich
      above green breath
among white testimonies
of lost time
tenderness of eyes
      never forgotten

MACDONALD PASS

late october
    and cold
with a leaping wind
begging its way
through the branches
    of leafless trees
long icy journey
over macdonald pass
    continental divide
    deep canyons
    of pine trees
    covered with snow
steep cliffs
    of gray rocks
        only time
moving west
down solemn slopes
down drifting dreams
    of prehistory
along the little blackfoot river
    south of mullan pass

narrow cautious trail
of wagon trains
    cattle grazing
        on frosty grass
fog
    in the valleys
floating over
      high haystacks
    surrounded by wooden fences
long-tailed magpies
    black and white
across rambling surfaces
       of death
a neutral measure
of timid essence
    blackfoot river
    and the angry
      architecture
    of missoula

SUNRISE

processional
depths
of sunrise
encourage
someplace patterns
of morning
corrupt
with caution

HOMESTEAD

hesitant sun
dark clouds
rude mountains
twisted patterns of barbed wire
lead to an abandoned homestead
on the little prickly pear creek
    wooden gate smashed
        into the ground
    low weather-scarred animal sheds
        empty and dilapidated
    hunks of rotting leather
    rusty horseshoes
        by the barn
        antlers above the door
empty cabin
    empty corral
the substance of the old west is gone
only legends remain

WINDOW FACES

a black
and
passing train
delivers
a portion
of the silent
and sinister faces
that haunt
the windows
of the world
in participation
and suppression
faces that know too little
faces that know too much
the broken mirrors
of narcissistic rage
hypnotized by motion
and ubiquitous
in their vigilance
squared in glass
in a moving museum
there
but in no official histories
voyagers
on an impossible
journey
no ticket refunds
no smoking
a kingdom of glass
concentrated in equal parts
without
a crown
of thorns
eyes cancel eyes
not enough light

to read
and conversation
is dead
soon they will be gone
leaving only the word
croatoan
carved on a door post
planning great strategies
without tactics
in parallel catharsis
fear and guilt
through a glass millennium
by a paper schedule
faces in motion
lost motion
without
the innocence
of huck's raft
lost motion
evil engines
abolish
earlier visions
despite
the many warnings
now
a calvary
and the agony
of window faces
candles of meditation
faces arranged
for less public occasions
reserved
for aediles
and long interregnum
of fragments
and a moral obligation
to lower shades
or wear masks

BUILDING

gothic revival
in slow death

two turrets
of smoke-black stone

hang on the corner
of a crumbling building

touching
cloud-flaked sky

gathering breaths
of sunlight

between windy groans
of decay

chipped gargoyles
with eternal scowls

perch on ledges
in quiet neglect

dark windows
smile

with teeth
of broken glass

endless stream
of morning traffic

speeds past
with stuttering noise

indifferent
to a relic

of chicago's
childhood

SWINGS

rusty swings
on the school playground

seatboards
broken out

only
long chains

hanging
solemnly

from a cold
steel bar

moved occasionally
by the wind

SECOND VERSION

nine o'clock nothing
in morning noose
lonesome dogs
left whining
in empty doorways
    square possession
    of brick notice
    and wide windows
bells and clocks
dreams and walks
anvil reasons
of ambitious time
denied seasons
of stolen time
angled facts
feeding fictions
    graven images
    chalked and cursed
    graveled civilization
    gifted by iron fences
doubtful diagrams
distance in distance

a room of chairs
voices in voices
a funnel of rooms
a book-clamped house
of tyranny and kindness
     spinning faces
     merging colors
a carrousel journey
in an empire of surfaces
     notes from home
     and calculations
     of quick exit
     solemn and singing
an ending pattern
a black mark
on the attendance register
expanding eyes seized
by high stone bridges
motion solved by thought
the whispering escape
down the parallel pardon
of railroad tracks
     running
   from the wishes
   of their claws

ACCUSATION

a weary chart
made weak
by walking points
of disloyalty
shouting ribbons
sacrificed
and forgotten
the lingering crisis
the present plague
loved for suffering
and pierced
by categories
back to nature
back to god
back to back
postcard tactics
tabled moss
quiet where
i saw privilege
roomed of age
hiding from choice
in slender scream
in moving watery
blackmail of memories
a far reluctance
a bad name
a righteous prophet
cage eyes
short of centuries
late lies
in rain and rage

LOGARITHMIC SONGS

a few notes
of clever music
form the axis
of a new galaxy
full of answers

with every
opposite vision
tenaciously held
in a summer vise
of rising smoke

lingering
on the dark edge
of quiet history
polishing skeletons
of ancestral folly

with every
fabled face locked
in synthetic stare
as crude voices
arrive in shouts

begging
for an audience
of patient ears
to listen
and approve

MOUNTAIN MEADOW

insect castle stump
below squirrel chatter

the wind through
pine trees

high thin clouds
time through time

bubbling symphony
of delicate sound

shallow stream flowing
through dandelion hills

narrow water rushing
over shining pebbles

rock slide sun
in fern silence

white animal skull
in dry bushes

chipmunk on log
above soft mulleins

brown explosions
of growth

at the end
of pine branches

small patches
of cold clover

dark green
along stream bank

aspen leaves in yellow
spin of autumn

SOUNDS

precise concerto
absorbs
slow sunset

i choke
in the thick
air
of reverence

my ears
follow
fierce wind

through
branches
of a tall
elm tree

a dead bough
dislodges

and falls
to earth

beethoven
smiles

BLOODSTONE

a rebellious colony
of collected forms
sitting in the gallery
lost in material sleep
a monday of symbols
a position of systems
a promise of theories
observation changes
both observer
and observed
diffraction patterns
prove nothing
since waves
of all matter
suppress lexicons
and a flawless approach
to retreat
is to think about thinking
while distant music
never quite clear
floats into hot rooms
from beyond the blackened gate
offering a wandering escape
relieving the scholastic burden

of the over-soul
and the charade
of pencil-making
sailing great caravels
on a small pond
enjoying the exhibition
of paradox
no interpretations needed
no reliable witnesses
fences painted
with old philosophy
where phoenix eggs
are eighty-nine cents
a dozen
and spiritual lynch mobs
with ropes
of false architecture
pray for resurrection
in order to kill again

THE ROOM

a wild room catches
the rushing rumors
of smoke-generous
official ignorance
delivered to tombs
in loose patterns
beyond cold motives
of envious duration
ball fringe drapes
vanishing into time
as color is stolen
by soft confessions
of a september sun
mozart dying slowly
on a wind-up victrola
enclosed bookcases
with empty shelves
speaking of dust
and a broken pencil
convenient voices
quickly finding
curved furniture

a raven's tapestry
singing faded chains
around elusive walls
pale ionic-columned
marble fireplace
obsessed with ashes
inventing dimensions
of secret anguish
and crowded isolation
the flag-waving
surrendered record
of shy experience
arguing and hoping
in deletive rotation
the growing burden
of early grievances
cut into sad smiles
by the stone ax
of consoling assurance

EXPLANATIONS

in the region of candles
they talked in small voices
about a black whale
on a white flag
  the contemplation
  of creation
and the web of epigrams
purchased by pieces
of cruel evidence
  language of debt
victims of village conclusions
   delicate chorus
a hand reaching out
a wind-tormented tree
a photon striking an electron
  two particles
  of self
museum-posed
words wearing emotion
emotion wearing words
pattern
 and fragment
the periodic table
of a mystic's chemistry
where life and art combine
to construct the soul

POSSIBILITIES

clusters
of grapes

paused
in purple

tangle
of vines

windward
eyes

scent
of pines

time
impaled

on grassy
spines

shift
of season

faded forest
finding

moments
of treason

shaded road
through

a sleepy
village

cut by
greedy hands

in iron
pillage

empty
rocking chairs

on paint-chipped
porches

afternoons
of caution

with begging
torches

poised
to deliver

red
and yellow

along
the reach

of autumn
river

DEBATE

"With their astounding glamour,
Whatever ghost one wished to hear,
By strange coincidence, was near
To make the past or future clear,
(Sometimes in shocking grammar)."
                                        —James Russell Lowell

quick towers
    of status and profit
secular chapel
    of an almost church
shepherds must leave
            their sheep outside
    expediency
of folding metal chairs
        when the collection plate
        is passed
put in two historical processes
        and take out
        your change

each speaker
carried history's weapons
    to slay
        contemporary politics
    and leave
        a personal altar
        in the smiling void
vultures perched
    on the edge
    of their chairs
waiting to sweep
down upon
    unprotected words
the jeers
    of mocking participants

the cheers
of prime communicants

socrates drunk
in the corner
practicing
his spontaneous laugh
loyal students
who
know the liturgy
by heart
prepare
the appropriate responses

analysis and forgery
the luxury
of complexity
the splendid syllogism
the missing empiricism
the fourth of july people
with frozen minds
syntax of doom
so sure
of final designs
depositing
evaporating rhetoric
purgatorial scorn
no opponents tolerated
how far does
pride precede a fall
will i have time
to abandon the temple
before it collapses
on me

which side won
oh that was
determined ages ago
we all won

LULLABY OF HIERONYMUS BOSCH

nearly eleven
o'clock

west harrison
street

quick-changing
shadows

under flashing
neon lights

of cheap
hotels

sharp jealous
sounds

of breaking
bottles

and coughing
curses

angrily
lulling

wine-soaked
strangers

into
the lonely

fatal clutch
of dreams

FALL AND WINTER

two miles across the bridge
where small gardens
    paraded beans
in warmer hours
    and rows of corn
    run toward
    the river
i watch time reduce
    the forms
    of fall
thinking of life
    and death
looking through
black branches
of november trees
at the sun
    sinking
into the river

white waves of cold
steal motion
from the river
    and hang
a gallery of art
    delicate
beyond the touch

i search for the past
beside the velocities
    of red
forgetting tales
of southern sun
    finding
old colonial trails
cold and hard
    hammered
by the long blows
of winter's
cruel fist
that abolish
    aesthetic travel
    and hide
rough-edged errors
in the frozen tears
of a minimum universe

THE LABORATORY

midnight on a cold campus
science building aglow
with eager rooms of research
deep roots of expectation
      minor reason
      in genetic cage
linked to large doses
of decoded drugs
      and the science
      of brutality
so cleverly
designed to hold
the lonely pressure
of existence
      in noble balance
and keep all appointments
within the numbers of time

STREET ARTIST

cracked
and cautious
call

of a rusty
church bell
ripping

the silence
of summer
twilight

loosely-tied
bundle
of brushes

careless
pile
of rags

cans
of paint
by a wall

finished wonder
late
with logic

but still
the only
way

CANVAS FROM ABYSSINIA

against old wood
and broken glass
below appreciation
above disparagement
hiding from the wind
on a sunday morning
we stood patiently
the cat and i
in a narrow doorway
in perpetual levels
of voluntary ritual
waiting for the rain
to wash the streets
and make a rainbow
each waiting quietly
tracing the future
in pools of water
on the sidewalk
listening to laughter
of ambiguous ancestors
meanings from meanings
each with orphan eyes
each an impenetrable world
until a dog arrived
wet and rowdy
to chase the cat
across the deserted street
down a frequent alley
into the shadows
of a cold afternoon
leaving me alone
in the rain
to invent
new strategies

BLUE HERONS

early spring in nebraska
giant wings
    against
        gray sky
blue herons
returning
from south america
    curved neck
    yellow eyes
cautious hunt
beak thrust
pierces calm surface
of shallow water
    a fish dies
wings flapping
    in dances
    of love
blue-green eggs
in a treetop nest
    a brood hatches
    and begins
    to learn

DANCE OF SHIVA

high waterfalls return
to their reason
a quality of violent
missionary motion

immense bays of foggy
swirling shores
command cold wind
to touch the face

intense prayer
sacred dream
dance of shiva
at moments when

the primal source
the all
hides and surrounds
the if

always released in
rhythmical screams
the six canons
of hsieh ho

the harbor of lights
cranes and masts
requesting
old memories

the ink tones
that if true
begin
the is

IN THOSE SHADOWS

at three owls past midnight
when the candles are lighted
in little corners of destruction
the flickering glow reveals
the contemptuous contour
of surrender's smile
hanging on the edge
of darkness
wide and obdurate
in the savage spaces
of motion
where wishes wash themselves
in tears
and parading prophets
put on sunglasses
to protect their eyes
from angry visions

ANGELS IN A TREE

angels in a tree
at peckham rye

ezekiel stumbling
across a field

the soul rising
through the ceiling

perception is not
locked

by the organs
of perception

street ballads
lost child

lamb and tyger
in a zoo

contraries
and progression

the ancients
the stoning of achan

is there
is there
   again

THE LICHENS

desperate
lichens

hang on
rough rocks

in a mountain
pass

the sun
explores

their yellow
orange

and red
touch

the wind
passes by

without
a glance

FACT

the separate symbols
of interpreted form
streak the mind

like april raindrops
rolling down
a window pane

——tomorrows flash
in the dark night
of memory

THE SNAKE

rocky hillside
afternoon sun

sudden noise
rattlesnake

five feet
of coiled rage

i quickly draw
my revolver

cock the hammer
and take aim

the sun flashes
on the gun barrel

two victims poised
in judgment

two organisms
in suspended time

both ready
to deliver death

a fang-piercing
slow painful death

a quick tearing
death of lead

arriving
at 800 feet per second

eyes finding eyes
all motion examined

life clings
to life

edge of life
edge of death

complete power
no motive

doubt subtracted
from caution

suspicious truce
purchasing escape

i step back
slowly

gun lowered
hammer uncocked

returned
to its holster

we depart
in different directions

THE STARS

"Where now is Homer, who possessed
the throne?"
                —Lucretius

        the clouds
        break apart
        and are blown
        eastward by
        the roaring
        wind

        a pack
        of stars
        prowls
        across the sky

UTRILLO'S STREETS

time has been destroyed
on the worn cobblestones
of utrillo's streets

below wooden shutters
closed over large
leering windows

below white towers
lost in the pale
paris sky

time has been destroyed
for those vague passengers
on their cobblestone voyage

who gradually grew out
of the artist's brush
to become themselves

BEAR MOUNTAIN

black aspen leaves
above sun-shattered
patches of snow

pond surface covered
with pine needles
pounded by rain

A RIDE ON THE DESCARTES FERRIS WHEEL

spiral of paradoxes
chases the mirror
of self
like a hangman's
posse
circling inward
but never quite
reaching
the hanging tree
of absolute zero

each half cut
fraction of known
and knowing
draws the searcher
deeper into
the tunnel
of sum and number
and precise self
the self
the self

the self
sinks
into the object
of its quest
which is its
own final image
and the laugh
of mystical
mathematicians
echoes and echoes
and echoes

one
round-trip
ticket-punched
all

THE BLACKFOOT RIVER

a small spider speeds
across pine cones
chunks of driftwood
and white stones
and crawls up
the steep clay
river bank

a piece of driftwood
tossed back into
the river

the scraping crunch
of footsteps
on the pebble shore

a driftwood plank
(from a miner's cabin
or mountain bridge
or ranch shed
or gold-greedy
sluice box)
water-rounded edges
nail holes
of some lost purpose

DREAM

"I sette not a straw by thy dreminges,
For swevenes been but vanitees and japes.
Men dreme al-day of owles or of apes,
And eke of many a mase therwithal;
Men dreme of thing that never was ne shal."
                              —Geoffrey Chaucer

self and object
discipline of vision

chair and table
forest memory

high-collared coats
and hair ribbons

sound and silence
before and after

dreamers of truth
sent by seasons

motives emerge
from instinct

and knowledge
fades into laws

SUNFLOWERS

explosions of white clouds
in bright blue
morning sky

tall black-eyed
wind-waving yellow flowers
arched to the ground

a rough faith
that derives
its surface salvation

from the plotting
intensity
of the sun

and the deep-rutted
road that runs
through the wish

THE DAKHMAS

vultures sweep into
seven years' silence
of desert dream

withered priests tend
the holy flame
in odor of incense

the morning is greeted
with fresh plants
and silver cups of water

rose petals drift
through pale pillars
of desert tombs

love-molded legends
starved and tortured
explode in reasons

trembling stars record
a small kindness
never repaid

BLUEBIRD

uncertain sun
in bluebird
wish

gray clouds
in cold thought
of broken branch

bluebird
sweeps over
barbed wire
fence

——it begins
to rain

THE SWORD

easily ransomed
by the coins
of fat machines
whiskey-armored
crusaders move
(recruiting poster confidence)
sideways through
concrete fields
of blood
choking on systems
of classification
(a dream slips into a myth)
watching merciless worlds
lure the senses
to the edge
of knowledge
(a flower for your grave)
demanding the plunge
into roaring
dimensions
of symbolic wisdom
(how many ways can
the same thing be said)

in order to mimic legends
and institutionalize terror
leering doctors
(certified by church
country club and political party)
relentlessly prescribe
a modest dose

of erotic mysticism
for the benefit
of art (next to motherhood
and democracy the noblest cause)
the shapes of temples
betray the ideas
sold within
(every sale needs to be
properly advertised)
and the boy scout handbook
states that if the ark capsizes
you should hang on and wait
for someone to come to the rescue
(while waiting to be rescued
recite the old pirate curse
"damn your eyes _____"
filling in the blank
with the names
of all your enemies)

it must be somewhere
(that lost happiness
nobody wants to find
or even talk about)
lost or hidden
in a fastidious ecstasy
hysterical and blind
marked by the corrosive
power of thrashing guilt
and all the standard
motionless colors
of hopeful camouflage
(safe in tunnels of ignorance

and sealed in anxious sounds
of fraud-discovered amazement)
hiding intoxicated bystanders
with the odor of cheap wine
flowing from the endless
architectural dreams
of frantic fountains
inside the mournful spaces
of ambitious genealogy
where freshly painted
patterns of revenge
twist the perceptions
of phlegmatic tourists
photographing the splendor
of submission
a slight resemblance
of our leaders
to hooded medieval executioners
goes unnoticed
(but then who has time
for such suspicious priestcraft
when the inflationary trend
of prophecies
is capturing even
our most sacred newspapers)
in other words
ladies and gentlemen
we are on trial
for our lives (and souls)
with no perry mason magician
to crawl out of a sustained objection
and save us
yet the tears conceal
a deeper journey
(we were doomed long ago

by the clocks and claws
in our evolution)

several miles beyond the city
we look back
and turn into salt
it doesn't matter
the view was stolen
by billboards
informing us of the nature
of our enemies
it is a too-late knowledge
because by the time you see the sword
it has struck